NAN BRADLEY

The
Arkansas
Traveler

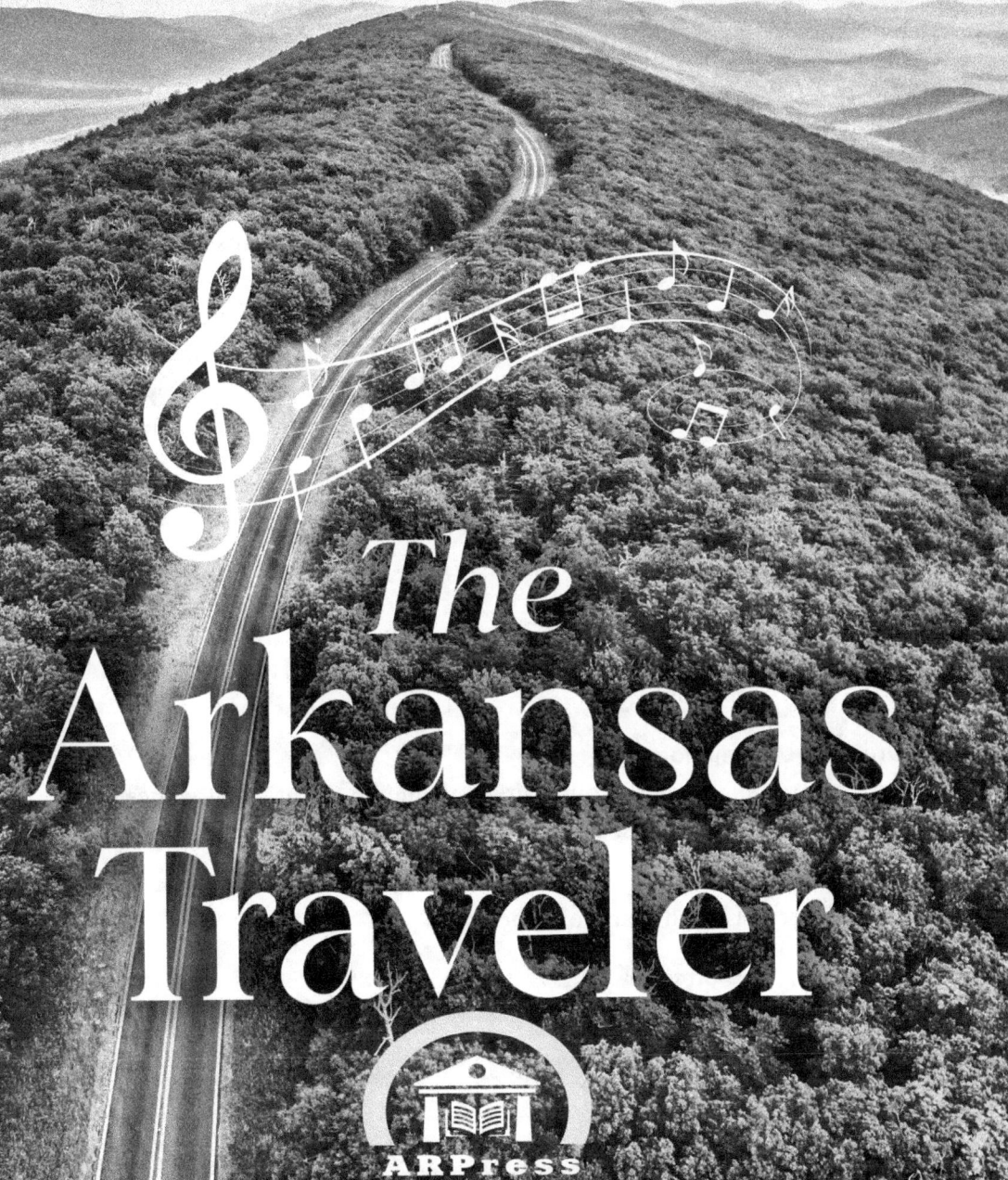

NAN BRADLEY

The Arkansas Traveler

ARPress
ILLUMINATING IDEAS
EMPOWERING VOICES

ARPress
45 Dan Road Suite 5
Canton, MA 02021

Hotline: 1(888) 821-0229
Fax: 1(508) 545-7580

Ordering Information:
Quantity sales. Special discounts are available on quantity purchases by corporations,associations, and others. For details, contact the publisher at the address above.

Printed in the United States of America.

ISBN-13:   Softcover   979-8-89389-885-9
            eBook   979-8-89389-886-6

Library of Congress Control Number: 2024923861

These parodies will seem rather childish and perhaps silly unless the reason or occasion for each one is known. When I first decided to leave the teaching profession in 1941, I went north to Ohio, and after Pearl Harbor, I went to work in a Defense Plant. At first the fact that I was from Arkansas made me the object of considerable kidding, some of which was not flattering. The only effective way I knew to kid back was in poems and songs. I wrote parodies, using familiar tunes so my ideas could quickly understood. I succeeded far better than expected. After a few months I not only was accepted but looked up to as the official poet and "Bard of the Building".

One of my first efforts was a friendly protest against a very disagreeable job in what was called the Knock-Off Bay. Here liquid TNT was poured into 75MM projectile casings and when it had cooled enough to be solid, the aluminum filler funnels has to be knocked from the top of the projectiles. The work was not easy and the dust and fumes from the TNT were both disagreeable and injurious. The tune used was: "Deep in the Heart of Texas." The song was popular and soon was heard all over the building which was known as the Loadline. For some reason or I was transferred from this particular job.

Deep In The HEART Of The KNOCK-OFF

Just hear that moan as they sweat and groan
Deep in the Heart of the Knock-Off
The work is tough and the speech is rough
Deep in the Heart of the Knock-Off.

Well I rue the day when I heard 'em say
"Report down to the Knock-Off".........
And if I had known how things went on,
I'd a tried to knock their block off.

So listen, Boys, no one enjoys
The work down the Knock-Off
And you can bet you'll sure regret
If you don't steer clear of the Knock-Off.

Not all the poems and songs were meant to be funny. This one was selected as the R.O.P. plant song. (RAVENNA ORDINANCE PLANT). It was published in the plant magazine and sung by request over the Warren, Ohio radio network. The tune is *"I've Been Working On The Railroad."*

I'VE BEEN WORKING ON THE LOADLINE

I've been working on the Loadline
All the livelong day
Working for The Atlas Powder.......
And the good old U.S.A.
Don't you hear the shells a 'rolling
Rolling toward the sea
And with vengeance they're extolling
"V" for VIC TO RY.

(Atlas Powder Co. was
the company in charge
of the plant)

Night and day we keep 'em rolling
To our comrades brave
For the Foe is still controlling
The land we seek to save
And unless we all endeavor
To fulfill our share
Freedom's cause is lost forever
And we shall feel despair.

So keep 'em rolling, keep 'em flying
By Air and Land and Sea
The World on us is now relying
To save Democracy...
We must never cease our labors
Though the night be long......
Till we help our suffering neighbors
To end the rule of wrong.

When I was transferred out of the Knock-Off Dept., I was given a job helping process T N T. This was shipped into the plant in flake form. There it was heated on steam heated grids until it became liquid. From a reservoir which was steam heated to keep the T N T at a constant temperature we drew it off into rubber tubs with a sort of spout for pouring and which were suspended from a tram-rail for ease in moving from bay to bay. (room to room). An aluminum paddle was used to stir the liquid to cool it. When it became thick and pasty the contents of the tubs were poured into rubber pails and then poured into the empty 75 MM projectile casings. Needless to say cleanliness in this dept. was imperative. Two men worked together. One did the stirring and the other kept the floor clean. The T N T was often splashed out upon the floor, but it crystalized instantly, like hot liquid sugar, and was easily scraped from the floor with a beryllium metal scraper which was non-sparking. A broom, a long handled scraper and a wet mop and pail were my tools. My partner and I loved to sing as we worked and as the song *"Walking The Floor Over You"* was very popular at the time I thought it would be fun if I could come up with a parody on it. The result was *"Mopping The Floor Over You"*.

When I had it ready I walked up to him one morning just as we started to work and said in pretended anger:

Now, Brother, you listen to this song
You know doggone well you done me wrong
You get the floor all dirty and I never do get through
Moppin the floor over you.

Chorus

I'm Moppin the floor over you
I can't keep it clean that is true
I'm sweeping and a scrapin and I never do get through
Moppin the floor over you.

You left me and you went away
You slipped off into the other bay
And right behind you left me working hard and feelin blue
Moppin the floor over you

I'm Moppin the floor over you
I can't keep it clean that is true
I'm sweepin and a scrapin and my back breaks right in two
Mopping the floor over you.

Now maybe you think that I don't care
That I'll go ahead and do your share
But, Brother, you're mistaken and I tell you I am through
Moppin the floor over you.

I'm Moppin the floor over you
I can't keep it clean that is true
I'm sweeping and a scraping and my back breaks right
in two Mopping the floor over you.

About this time I realized that I was not only homesick, but I missed very much the boys and girls with whom I had spent so much time in the class-room, in sports, and in community activities. These two songs came into my mind. The first one I'll have to list as a poem. The tune was also mine and I have no proper paper to set down the notes. The second one is a parody written to the tune: *"Renfro Valley"*.

HOME

I am thinking today of a home far away
And my heart fondly dreams of the time
When my work will permit me to return to it
And the dear folks I left behind.

I was anxious to roam when I left that old home
For I thought that the world offered more;
But I now realize pleasure that money buys
Can't replace what I had before.

How I long every day for the young folks so gay
That I thought how to study and play
They have captured my heart and when life let us part
It would not try to get away.

So here's love to that home and the friends that it gave
May God bless them and keep them the same;
And allow me some day to go back there to stay
And again hear them call my name.

Take Me Back To DIXIE

There's a place for which I'M yearning
Though it's very far away
And my heart with love is burning
For the folks I miss today.
Time cannot erase the memories
Of the days that used to be,
When I lived at home in Dixie
With the folks I long to see.

I was happy way down yonder
But my spirit longed to roam
And I started out to wander
Strayed away from Home, Sweet Home.
Other places I found pleasant
Other people I found kind;
But my heart is still in Dixie,
With the folks I left behind.

Take me back to dear old Dixie,
I desire no more to roam;
How my weary heart affects me,
Far away from Home, Sweet Home.
Time cannot erase the memory
Of the days that used to be
When I lived at home in Dixie,
With the folks I long to see.

Of course, at this time there was throughout the plants indeed throughout the whole nation a great drive to persuade people to buy savings bond and stamps. We expressed our feelings to the tune of Alexander's Ragtime band..

Come on in here, come on in here,
Uncle Sam's appeal to you
Come on in here, come on in here,
What he wants us to do.....
There's a job for everybody and we mustn't let him down,
We serve him in the factory, on the farm and in the town
We'll back the boys on land and sea and in the air..
We'll buy his bonds, we'll buy his stamps
We'll raise the revenue,
We'll pay the price and sacrifice
We'll see all glory through
When the clouds roll by and peace has come
We'll be thrill to see.....
A victory for liberty, and freedom everywhere!

The area in which I was working was filled with a polyglot population, partly because of nearby steel mills and partly because this was a huge defense plant and drew employees from all over the northeastern part of the country, which included New York and Pennsylvania. There were Poles, Czechs, Italians, German, Greek, even Russian. A great favorite song was: *"Beer Barrel Polka"*. One day, one of My Italian friends asked me to make up a song to this tune. At first I thought that would be about as difficult a tune as I could use but the words came much easier that I had expected.

ROLL OUT THE BOMBER

Cho: Roll out the Bomber
Roll out the Tank and the Gun;
Just keep 'em rolling
We've got the Foe on the run.
Roll up Old Glory
Let her ever wave with the sun,
We're a gonna write our own finish
To what they've begun.

Pearl Harbor!Pearl Harbor!
That's where they made their error
We're not forgetting the deed committed there;
MacArthur, MacArthur,
That name fills them with terror,
On him we're betting a
And with him goes our prayer.

But there is work to do for everyone
Our sacrifices, too, have just begun;
We must not shirk or slight our duty
Or Freedom's cause may not be won.
This is the time that counts, it's now or never,
The rule of Terrorism now must cease......
We'll break the Tyrant's power forever,
And liberate the Dove of Peace.........

Chorus

One of the most unusual requests I received for a song was from an exceptionally good-natured young colored boy, who worked in my department at the time, and who was a favorite with everyone around him. Since we were both from the South and nearly everyone else around was from the Northern part of the country, we were very close friends. The song I wrote for him was no parody but my own tune. It described him so well that it was a very popular hit with all our friends.

"Carefree Daddy From Caroline"

I'm a carefree Daddy Caroline,
I ain't got no Blues.
When I crossed that Mason-Dixon Line
Every heartache every tear,
Every worry, every care;
I'm gonna look for Sunshine everywhere,
Like I had in Caroline.

I'm a carefree Daddy from Caroline,
Troubles leave me be
When I left that old hometown of mine
I just had to see......
Every thing that Time and Fate
Would permit and tolerate;
I gotta move on, I can't hesitate
Cause I'M missing Caroline.

I'M a carefree Daddy from Caroline,
I don't worry none.
Ain't got no time to fret and pine,
I'm a'gonna have my fun......
I like everybody and I want lots of Friends,
I'm gonna stay good natured till this old Life ends;
On the Boy From Caroline.

I'm a carefree Daddy from Caroline,
And I want the World to know;
When UNCLE SAM says, "Fall in Line",
I'm all set to go......
I want to see OLD GLORY waving high
Everywhere I go and until I die;
And when she needs me I'll be standing by......
And I want the World to know.

I had not been working in the Loadline many months when I developed T N T poisoning. The fumes and dust, no matter how well controlled, were too much for me (as well as many others), and I had to be transferred to an area where proximity to the product was not necessary.

Since the plant dealt in explosives, the buildings and facilities were located very far apart. In fact, the Reservation on which the plant was located measured ten miles by thirteen miles. The headquarters for the Dept. For Inspection of Inert Materials was located in building number 808. The dept. was called, simply, 808. This was where I was sent. Here the members of the inspection staff had an office of their own, separate from that of the head of the dept. They also had access to company vehicles for making their rounds, which sometimes meant visiting areas several miles apart. The badge worn was honored at any building in any area. This all added up to prestige, and the members of this group were inclined to be a little smug and cocky.

I came to 808 well recommended, but I was not too well received at first. I was considered green intruder, trying to become a part of the elite. I sensed this and didn't help matters any with my corny jokes. In order that I might get acquainted and at the same time become familiar with my new duties I was sent out each day with a different inspector. After several days of this, the superintendent called us all into his office one morning as we started to work and said to me:

"Mr. Pippen, I believe you've been out with every member of our staff now, is there anyone whose name you don't know?" Innocently, I replied, "Oh, I know everyone here." But I have never been able to figure out this fellow "Gage." The superintendent was very perplexed and said with surprise, "Why, we don't have a Mr. Gage in our department." I explained, "Well, everyday when we get ready to leave for work you tell us not to forget to take BURLEY GAGE. I never have been able to figure out who you mean."

Poor balls. With the helpless feeling of dealing with the hopeless, he opened a disc drawer and pull out a large gauge or measuring the OD of 24OMM shell casings. This he said, "This is what I meant" the gauge was for checking the largest dimension of the projectile, all the bourrelet, pronounced, burr lay. This was important that this dimensions the accurate to make sure the shell did not stick in the gun when it was fired.

For the next couple of weeks I was tolerated but not accepted. I kept poking fun at every opportunity. One day one of the men looked at me sharply and said, "I've just come to the conclusion that you've been pulling our leg." From that moment on I was "in". Before long we were a closely knit group and became wildly known for our warm friendship for each other and our dedication to our work. I was selected to be the coordinator between the men and the superintendent to expedite our work. We triggered congressional investigation with some of the big companies supplying materials to our plant complained vigorously to the government that our inspections were unfair and too severe.

A Committee was sent to conduct an investigation. This was an awesome thing for my boss to face. He almost became a mental case, brooding about it. He knew we were thorough and he was afraid we had gone overboard in our enthusiasm. He had left the checking of most of the reports to me and he had no idea how bad the rejected materials really were. To make matters worse, he had to conduct the Committee on their tour. It was my assignment to go ahead of the group, locate and conspicuously mark the products in question. When it was all over our dept. was completely vindicated and our boss received a special commendation. The companies involved were severely reprimanded and their contracts threatened if corrections were not made immediately. Future supplies from these companies were almost flawless.

From that moment the boss trusted us, implicitly.

One of my brainstorms that didn't endear me to my boss but highly amused my companions came about in this manner: We worked six days but not on Sunday. Each Sat. from mid-night to 8 A.M. one of us stayed in our office to take care of any emergency inspections that might have to be made in the name of safety, or otherwise. Since we only had to go out when called by phone, most of our time we spent sleeping on a tabletop. During one, the nights I had to work this shift I had to go to the rest-room. Un-knowingly, I left my keys on the table.

When I went out the door closed and locked automatically. In order to get back in I had to drive several miles to the Plant Security Headquarters and god I plant guard to take a pass key and unlock my office door. Of course I knew the Security Dpt. would standout a report to all departments concerned, especially my own, so I entered the following report in the log we were required to keep..

I was forced to be gone from the office for 5 or 10 minutes in the fact the I bother to lock it resulted in plenty of woe. The keys were entirely forgotten until I find time to return. Then with a shock I discovered a fact most unnerving to learn; inside most serene on the table dear little creatures were repost and I was completely unable to open the door that was closed.

Please don't be too severe in your judgement! I implore you please don't rub it in! I swear this is one situation I hope will never occur again!!!

It was at 808 that my spirits soared to their greatest heights while working at R O P. Also it was there that my morale reached its lowest ebb. It all had to do with softball.

Softball was a mania at R O P and the season arrived soon after I started work at 808. There were enough teams for a league with two divisions and at the end of the season the winner of each division played for the championship. 808 was one of those teams. The other team was from the Plant Fire Dept. Each team had one ace pitcher and only one.

The one to win two games out of three would be champion. We lost the first game but won the second. Immediately following the first game The Fire Dept. team's best pitcher had to leave for induction into the Army. He was a tall, handsome colored boy and had the fastest pitch I have ever faced. With this pitcher lost to our opponents we were heavy favorites. We had our ace pitcher ready for the championship game and he was good. However the enemy's third string pitcher was stubborn. (and when I say enemy that's what I mean; the two teams were barely on speaking terms and to start a fight between fans was easy.) Going into the last half of the final inning the score was tied and we were at bat. Our pitcher was up first and managed to get on base. He had a crippled foot and had difficulty in running. Our manager asked for a substitute runner. Now in organized softball, as in baseball, this means the man getting a runner must.

Leave the game. This was gleefully pointed out by several players on the opposing team. This meant we were about to lose our best pitcher for the rest of the game.

Now getting a man on base in the last half of the last inning, with no one out is usually a sure win in softball. I was the next man up with orders to bunt. I was considered one of the most expert bunters in the league. The pitcher sent in a slow pitch. I expected a fast ball and went for the pitch too quickly. I popped it up to the pitcher who grinned from ear to ear and doubled the runner off first for the second out. Our chance to score had passed.

The game went into extra innings and continued without further scoring until it began to look like darkness would stop it. Finally the Fire Dept. got a man around to third base with one out. The next batter hit a fly ball to me that was not real deep. Normally, a runner can score easily on such a fly after the catch, but I was one of the few fielders in the league with a reputation for cutting down runners on just such.

A fly ball. The runners streak for home with a mighty heave I threw to the catcher, too hard! Instead of losing height as it speed in the ball was lifted by the air resistance and curved slightly to one side. The runner was safe! The Fire Department Team had finally broken the tie. They won the game. We couldn't score in our half of the inning and the championship had eluded us. I think I was probably the most rejected one of our team. I felt it my last throw in the last inning should have gotten the runner our catcher put his arms around my shoulder and said, "I have to agree that for you it was and error, for I've seen you make that throw too many times. But it wont go into the record book as an error because no one expects those of us on this thing. If only it could be done."

Sometime before, the manager of our team had asked me to write a poem or song about his team. A promise, was found difficult to get any ideals. But now I felt I must certainly write something quickly, to make up for my part in the loss of the championship. I was so upset that I couldn't sleep at night. Words and ideals begin to creep into my mind and I really had too many to make my pass easy. I couldn't forget a magnificent sportsmanship a manager of the other team displayed. Finally I had my theme! In the middle of the night I started writing and it was easy. I woke late the next morning. I didn't have time to eat and shave. I was bleary eye and presented a very disheveled appearance. I haunted my manager and gave him the poem and asked that he have a copy made and sent to the Chief of the Plant Fire Dept., a fiery, snow thatched little rooster of over seventy, who loved his softball team passionately. Before my manager would read the poem I slipped out of sight and managed to get to work without having to speak to anyone else. I meant to stay out of sight all day, come in late at the end of the shift and slip off home before anyone noticed how sloppy and unkempt I was. This is what I handed my manager and asked that he share with the sentimental old Fire Chief:

The FATE OF 8 0 8

Some teams are good, some teams are bad,
Some teams are second rate;
But listen to… the Waterloo
Of the team from 8 0 8.

Contenders through the season's fray
For laurels and acclaim
They met disaster on the day
They played the Final game.

Each team was good, each team was bad,
Their records parallel;
But each well worthy of the right
To hear the final bell.

The game was fast, the game was close,
Scarce any flaw was seen;
Performance was remarkable
The spirit fair and clean.

A normal game could not decide
Just who should wear the crown,
And on and on the battle raged
Til twilight settled down.

Then Fate grew weary of the fray
And deigned to cast her lot;
The one she favored now could win,
The one she spurned could not.

Meanwhile in one of the out of the way storage areas, I was trying to get the day over with, inconsistently. About 11 am the P.A. system (a part of all the building) called me back to our office. Miserably, I reported. The boss grind wickedly at my discomfiture. I had put him on the spot in mischief many times and now he was enjoying my embarrassment. I had been summoned, he told me, to appear at plant headquarters, immediately! I was terrified! On top of my original condition when I reported to work, my clothes were wrinkled and dirty. I had been climbing over dusty crapes all morning. Sternly, and gleefully my boss pointed out that his inspectors were expected to be neat and presentable at all times.

I reported to the main office as directed, I was ushered into a plush office and was embarrassed noticed who it was. The man behind the desk rose and greeted me. He had a copy of my poem in his hand. I was deeply puzzled. I wondered if I had done something unethical in sending the poem to the fire chief. I was afraid I had offended him. This was the last thing I wanted to happen. The man spoke;

"Mr. Pippen, this is a fine job. You certainly seem to have a way with words. In a few hours this poem has done more to eliminate friction and discord than we have been able to do in months. The Fire Chief requested that this be read over the Plant P.A. system. It has already been read twice and will be read on all three shifts. They tell me that when the Chief read your poem he cried. We would like to have you join our magazine staff and help us promote better Public Relations through your writing."

I was happy and flattered. Of course I agreed. Perhaps this was but a start. Was it possible that I was about to embark upon a career of writing? The idea appealed to me. but Uncle Sam soon put a crimp in that plan. A few days later he sent me his Greetings and invited me to join his organization.

There was an aftermath to the affair of the softball game that was totally unexpected and surprising. About a week after the game our manager stopped me and confided, "Pippen, this championship game is still being played from Akron to Youngstown. As the losing manager I am a Hero. They're praising me a lot more than if I had been the winning manager. Man, I'm famous." He shook his head in disbelief. "I don't get it. Beats me what it takes to get recognition."

I grinned happily, for the miracle had happened that I had dared hope for, but couldn't quite believe, myself.

Came the day when I was to finish at 8 0 8. Since it would be my last day there, I had expected to loaf and have a good time. There were others leaving for the Army, too, and it was customary to meet down at the local night club the night before having to leave for induction to celebrate with friends. I was looking forward to that night. (they served soft drinks, too.)

The boss changed my plans for an easy day. He said some very important work had piled up on him that only I could handle properly, and asked if I would take care of it for him. He made me feel so necessary that I cheerfully accepted the task. I didn't finish until late and when I got back to the office everyone had gone home but the boss. He handed me my paycheck, said hurriedly, "See you tonight," and rushed off. Just like that! Didn't even shake my hand. Didn't say any of the nice things I had expected him to say. And I thought he was my closest friend. Not even one of my fellow workers had stayed to say goodbye, and I was only a few minutes late. I was stunned. I could barely think. I stumbled to my car and drove home without knowing what I was doing. My wife, who had left to put the kids in school in Arkansas when I got my induction notice, had come back to Ohio to stay with me until I left for the Army. She tried to soothe my wounded pride. "Don't be such a fool about a job. It's not the end of the world! After all, maybe some of your gang will be at the club tonight.

Your boss talked like he was coming. But the boss and most of my friends lived too far away to be expected to show up for a few drinks, what with the gas rationing and all. I was almost broken hearted. I decided to stay at home, myself.

My wife is very practical and pointed out to me that if I failed to show up to tell the other inductees goodbye, I'd be treating them just like my plant buddies had treated me. That did it. I didn't want anybody to feel as deserted as I did right then. So my wife and I went to the club.

When we opened the door we saw the pace was crowded. There was a moment of silence then a deafening roar went up, and the crowd began to sing, "For He's a Jolly Good Fellow." At first I had no idea this was for me, but as my eyes began to get accustomed to the dark room, I realized that every member of my dept. was there, male and female, and many other friends and well-wishers. My wife and I were hustled to a long, crowded table, well supplied with food, and seated in two chairs waiting for us. Some one yelled, "Let's eat," and the party was on. A hundred years fell from my shoulders. My wife punched me and grinned, "Aren't you glad you came?" She had been in on the gag all the time. My boss had deliberately kept me busy in the field so the party could be planned. I thought nothing could add to my happiness at that moment. Everybody was shouting and talking at once and no one was making sense, but no one cared. It was a wild happy babble.

When the meal was over the boss signaled for quiet and stood up. He told how they had tricked me and had pretended to be indifferent. But he said I had it coming because I would have done them the same way if I had been given the same opportunity. Then he began to praise me and my work in the dept. until my face was red enough to light a fire. When he finished he presented me with a present, a very nice billfold. I stammered my thanks and started to put it in my pocket. "Open it!" they shouted in chorus. I looked inside and it was filled with money. Every member of my dept. had contributed liberally. I was overwhelmed. "Speech!" They cried. I got to my feet. For the first time since they had known me I was speechless. With tears streaming all I could say was "Thanks." They understood and cheered.

The magic of that moment will never leave me. To some people the expression 8 0 8 meant just a building. To me it had been a way of life. And it taught me a great lesson: Most people are softies at heart, and they can still be reached with WORDS.